ECHO DOT
3rd Generation

The Beginner to Expert Guide with Tips & Tricks to Master your Echo Dot and Troubleshoot Common Problems

Michael Philip

Copyright © 2019 by Michael Philip - All rights reserved.

all other copyrights & trademarks are the properties of their respective owners, Reproduction of any part of this book without the permission of the copyright owners is illegal-except with the inclusion of brief quotes in a review of the work.

CONTENTS

Introduction 1

How To Set Up The Amazon Echo Dot 4

How to Make Amazon Echo Understand Your Voice 9

How to Enable Alexa's Follow-Up Mode 12

What Is Alexa Voice Shopping, and How Do You Use It? 16

Amazon Alexa – Smart home 26

How to Connect a Nest Thermostat to Alexa 34

How to Connect Philips Hue Lights to Amazon Echo 39

How to Connect an Amazon Echo to a Harmony Remote 43

How to create an Amazon Echo stereo pair 48

How to add an Amazon Echo Sub and configure Alexa EQ settings
.... 52

Alexa Tips & Tricks 56

    Add Skills 56

    Group devices together 57

    Add routines 57

    Change your default music service 58

    Boost your music with two speakers (and a Sub) 59

Set multiple timers 59

Change the wake word 60

Make Alexa less annoying 61

Set an alarm 62

Get things done one after the other with Follow-Up mode 62

Enable Night Light 63

Add Email & Calendar 64

Create multiple profiles 65

Protect your purchases 66

Use IFTTT 67

Personalise your Flash Briefing 69

Say goodbye, Alexa 70

Top essential Alexa Skills to try first 71

How to set up and use Alexa smart home groups 81

How to make Alexa Routines – smart home automation made easy 86

How to make Skype calls with Amazon Alexa 92

Amazon Alexa – Drop in, calls and messages 96

Common Amazon Echo problems – and how to fix them quickly 99

The Wi-Fi connection is inconsistent or non-existent 99

Alexa won't connect to other devices 101

Alexa doesn't understand me 103

Alexa won't connect to my Bluetooth devices 104

Streaming services aren't … streaming 105

Reducing unwanted activations 106

Alexa Skills are playing up 107

All my Sonos speakers duck when I speak to Alexa 108

If all else fails… 109

Introduction

The Echo Dot is Amazon's small, puck-like smart speaker with the firm's Alexa voice assistant built in. New for the third generation is a softer, more rounded aesthetic with fabric sides. It is also slightly larger in all directions, measuring 99mm in diameter and 43mm tall.

At the back is a circular power socket, replacing the microUSB socket of the old Dot, and a standard 3.5mm analogue socket for connecting to a stereo. On top you have the volume buttons, action button and the microphone mute button.

You can also use Bluetooth to stream from the Dot to other speakers or from your phone or other device to the Dot to use it as Bluetooth speaker.

The updated design is joined by an improved speaker. The sound is fired out from the fabric sides of the new Dot, instead of the plastic top of the old model, projecting sound further into the room making it much better for music. The quality of the speaker has also been upgraded. It won't beat larger speakers, but for the money it sounds pretty good, edging out Google's Home Mini.

The mids are punchy, the highs relatively crisp and while there's no real bass to speak of, the new Dot sounds relatively rounded for a small speaker.

Feed it guitars and vocals from something like the live version of Hotel California by the Eagles from Hell Freezes Over and you're greeted with a warm, inviting tone. Classical tracks such as Jupiter from Holst's the Planets sound fairly rounded too. The Dot struggles with bass-driven electronica, but coped better than expected with Dr Dre's Still D.R.E. despite its pumping bassline.

The Dot can also get pretty loud, although not quite as loud as Google's Home Mini, and the audio starts to distort in high-energy tracks at maximum volume.

With smart speakers, the hardware you buy is only half the story: they live or die by the capability of the voice assistant within them.

The Dot's Alexa performance is first rate, with its four-microphone array being able to hear you over things like the cooker hood going full pelt in the kitchen or when playing music at maximum volume even if you do have to shout a bit. Alexa also sounds good through the Dot's speakers.

How To Set Up The Amazon Echo Dot

Setting up the Echo Dot only takes a few minutes, even if you're new to smart home devices. Here's how to get your Amazon Echo Dot up and running.

1. Download and open the Alexa app (Android and iOS) on your smartphone or tablet.

2. Select Devices in the lower right corner.

3. Press the Plus sign in the top right corner, or press the hamburger menu (the three horizontal lines) in the upper left corner

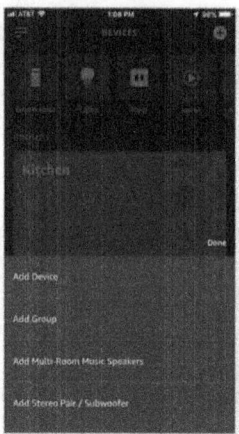

4. Select "Add Device."

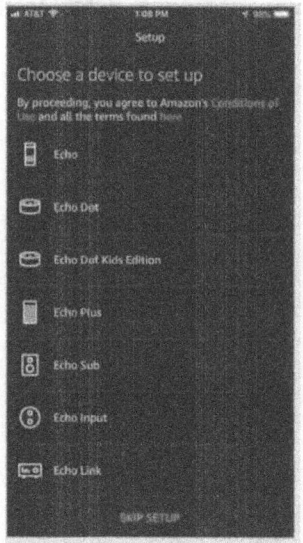

5. Press the Amazon Echo icon, followed by the Echo Dot icon that appears on the next screen. Then, press the image of the third-generation Echo Dot.

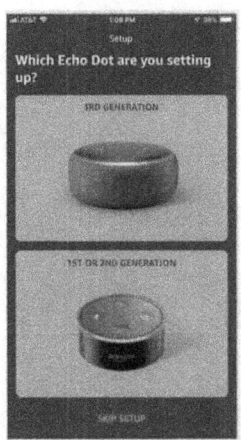

6. Plug in your Echo Dot using the included power adapter. Once the blue light ring has turned orange, your device is in Setup Mode.

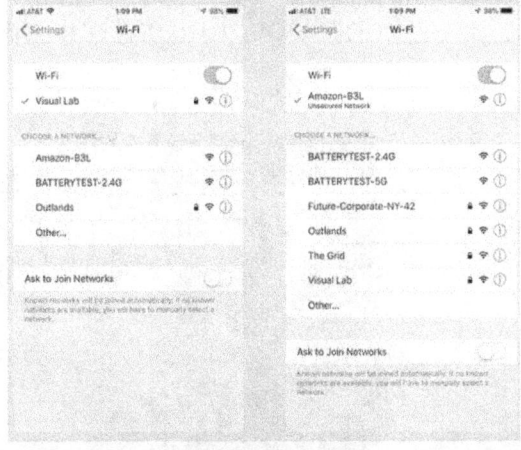

7. Wait for your Echo Dot to appear on your phone and select it. You'll be prompted to go to your Wi-Fi settings. Once there, select the

network called "Amazon-XXX." Then, return to the Alexa app.

8. Choose the Wi-Fi network to which you want to connect your Echo Dot. Enter your password if required.

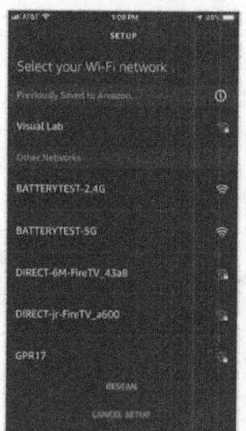

9. Select the external speaker your Echo Dot will be using. If you won't be connecting this device to an external speaker, skip this step.

10. Select the room where your Echo Dot is located (or create a new room).

Congratulations: You've set up your Echo Dot!

How to Make Amazon Echo Understand Your Voice

The Amazon Echo smart speaker is totally reliant on understanding your voice. But that doesn't mean it will understand every accent of vocal tick right out of the box. That's why Amazon built in some tricks to make it better learn your vocal inflections.

1. Open the Alexa app on your smartphone.

2. Tap the three bar menu button on the top left.

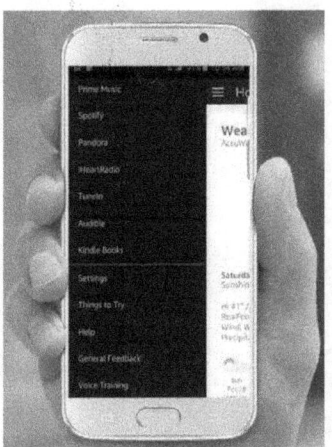

3. Scroll down and tap Voice Training.

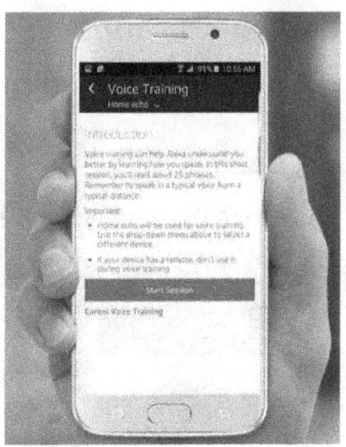

4. Tap Start Session.

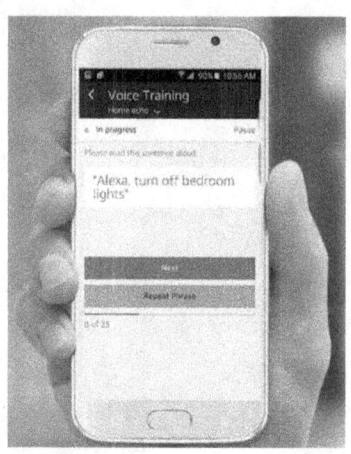

5. Get close to the Amazon Echo and say each of the 25 phrases that appear on the screen. After each tap Next.

6. Tap Start a New Session if you want Alexa to keep learning, or simply go to the home page.

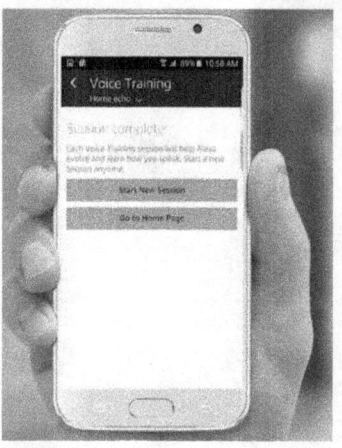

You can repeat this process if you notice a pattern of Alexa misunderstanding your commands. You can also see what Alexa heard in the app. If it's incorrect, tap No. This will continue you her education.

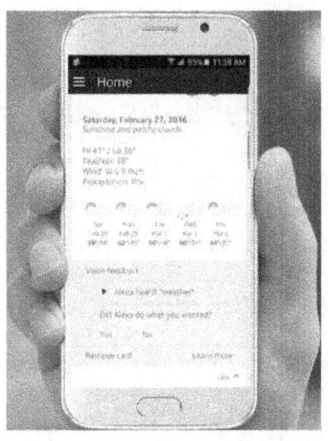

How to Enable Alexa's Follow-Up Mode

Tired of having to say "Alexa..." before every command to Amazon's voice assistant? A feature called Follow-Up Mode lets you make multiple requests without having to say the trigger word each time. When enabled, Alexa will keep listening — and the blue ring on your Alexa device will remain lit — for 5 seconds after she responds to your initial request.

So, for example, you can say "Alexa, set the thermostat to away mode." After she says OK, you can then say "turn the lights off," or some other command, like "lock the doors."

This feature is available for all Echo devices, and third-party devices such as the Sonos One, Garmin Speak Plus, GE Sol, and Ecobee4 thermostats. However, it's uncertain if Follow-Up Mode will work with all third-party Alexa devices. It also won't work if you're listening to music or making a call using Alexa.

First, though, you have to activate Follow-Up Mode for all of your Alexa-enabled devices individually. Here's how to do it.

1. Open the side menu from the home page of the Alexa app.

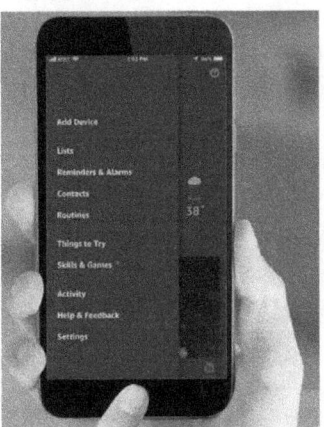

2. Select Settings. Then select Device Settings.

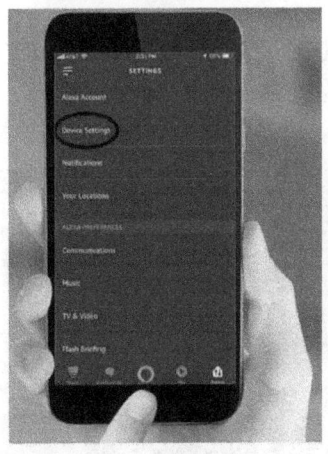

3. Choose an Alexa device. Scroll down and select Follow-Up Mode.

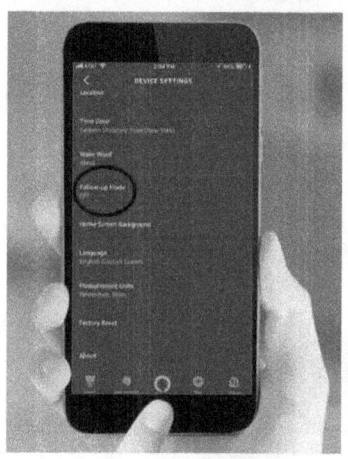

4. Press the slider to activate Follow-Up Mode. You will need to do this for every Alexa device you own.

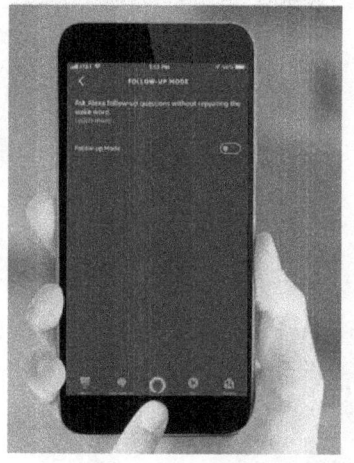

What Is Alexa Voice Shopping, and How Do You Use It?

Although voice shopping is still a nascent retail channel, studies show it's set to take off. As we approach Amazon Prime Day, more people than ever may be curious about the voice-assisted medium.

A recent survey by Sumo Heavy indicates that only 1 in 5 consumers has tried voice shopping. However, data suggests voice shopping will increase as digital assistants like Alexa and Google Assistant make their want into more homes. In fact, the industry expected to jump from the $2 billion industry it is today to $40 billion by 2022. Moreover, Amazon is expected to dominate the new channel with the largest market share of smart speakers, currently more than twice that of its competitors Google and Microsoft.

Amazon's Alexa Voice Shopping service lets you make purchases or get a rundown of the day's best deals with the sound of your voice. For instance, if you decide you need some paper towels, you can shout out your request to Alexa, and within days, your order will arrive at your doorstep.

The e-tailer has even offered exclusive Alexa-only discounts to consumers who purchase or re-order items via an Alexa device.

But there are some requirements you should know about. First, you'll have to be an Amazon customer, and you'll want to be a Prime member subscriber to make Alexa Voice Shopping much easier. You'll also need a device with Alexa built in, such as an Echo Dot.

If you can tick all those boxes, Alexa Voice Shopping might be a great alternative to brick-and-mortar stores and, yes, traditional online shopping.

What is Alexa Voice Shopping?

Alexa Voice Shopping is a service from Amazon that allows you to place orders through the online retail giant with just a voice command.

So, if you have an Alexa-enabled product, like an Amazon Echo or even the Amazon app for Android and iOS, all you have to do is tell Alexa what you want to buy. Alexa immediately searches Amazon to find the product and confirms it has picked the item you want. If you respond with a "yes," the order is placed.

On its Alexa Voice Shopping page, Amazon says you can choose from the millions of products it offers, and to help you save a few bucks, you can even ask Alexa what deals there might be on certain products.

Still not exactly sure how it might work? Here's a scenario:

Let's just say you've been parched all day, and you're drinking bottle after bottle of Fiji water. Suddenly, you realize you're all out. Rather than drive to the store in the scorching summer heat, you decide to order a case through Amazon and have it delivered to your house.

So, you say, "Alexa, order Fiji Natural Artesian Water." Alexa will hear that and will respond by telling you that it's found an option on Amazon for a certain price. Then, Alexa will ask you if it's OK to order. If you're happy with the product Alexa found, you can say "yes," and your order will be placed.

Now, sit back, relax and wait for your water to arrive.

Where can I find Alexa Voice Shopping?

One of the nice things about Amazon Alexa is that it's ubiquitous. The virtual personal assistant runs on a host of devices, allowing you to interact with it to search the web, place online orders and keep track of your schedule.

Here's a list of devices that are compatible with Alexa Voice Shopping:

- Amazon Echo
- Amazon Tap
- Amazon Echo Dot
- Amazon Fire TV
- Amazon Fire Tablets
- Amazon app (available on iOS and Android)

Can I ask Alexa sophisticated questions?

Yes, Alexa Voice Shopping can understand sophisticated queries. So, for example, you can ask for specific brands of household goods.

Say you have a particular coffee brand you like. You can order it through Alexa Voice Shopping by saying, "Alexa, order Newman's Own K-Cups." Alexa will find it on Amazon and facilitate the purchase.

Don't go easy on Alexa — the virtual assistant can handle it.

Do I need to be a Prime member?

Technically, Alexa Voice Shopping is available to anyone who uses the aforementioned Amazon hardware or software. However, if you're a Prime member, Alexa Voice Shopping is far more useful.

If you want to place orders through one of Amazon's devices, you must be a Prime member who has 1-Click ordering enabled. If you're not a Prime member and do not have 1-Click ordering turned on, you won't be able to access Alexa Voice Shopping from one of Amazon's many devices.

If you plan to try out the voice service through the Amazon app, however, all that changes.

From the Amazon app, you can search for and add an item to your cart with voice commands issued through Alexa Voice Shopping. Better yet, you don't need to be a Prime member or have 1-Click ordering turned on to do it.

If you want to buy whatever you put into your cart, though, you need to head back to your app and manually place your order.

What is Amazon's Choice?

When you haven't bought certain items before and you're simply looking for recommendations within the product category, Alexa Voice Shopping will return results from the company's Amazon's Choice line of products.

Amazon's Choice is a curated collection of products, across a wide array of categories, that have high ratings and solid prices. Think of the Amazon's Choice collection as Amazon's picks for the best products in its store.

While Alexa Voice Shopping will allow you to pick the product, Amazon's Choice gives you quick access to some of the best products on the service.

How do I set up a confirmation code?

Although it's nice to be able to quickly add a product to your cart and buy it, that won't be helpful if you don't want to make a purchase right away.

To address those situations, Amazon allows you to set up a confirmation code with Alexa. So, after you ask to add something to the cart, Alexa won't actually charge your card and process the transaction until you provide your four-digit code.

To set up the confirmation code, you need to launch the Alexa app and go to Menu > Settings. From there, you can choose Voice Purchasing and set a four-digit code.

Once that code is saved, when you place an order, Alexa will ask if you'd like to proceed with the purchase by providing your four-digit code. If you ignore Alexa, your order will remain in the queue and will not process until you're ready.

When you are ready to buy, simply tell Alexa your code.

OK, I goofed. Can I cancel a purchase?

If you made an accidental purchase, all is not lost. But you'd better move quickly.

If you ordered through Amazon's 1-Click, you have 30 minutes to cancel it before it's completed.

To cancel an order within the allotted time frame, go to your Amazon account, and click on Your Orders. There, you'll see a list of orders and the option, if applicable, to Cancel Items. Next, you can check the box next to each item you want to cancel. When you're done, click "Cancel checked items."

Your order is now canceled.

Can I order more than one item with Alexa Voice Shopping?

Well, yes and no.

If you're hoping to buy two different items in the same order, you won't be able to do so with Alexa Voice Shopping. Instead, each request for products will be its own order. So, if you want to buy a new phone charger, shampoo, water and chips, all four items will be listed in separate orders.

However, if you want to buy more than one of a certain item, you can. So if you want two bags of chips, you can request your quantity, and Alexa will take care of the rest.

You can also create a shopping list to make multiple purchases easier. To create a shopping list, go to the menu in the top left corner of the Alexa app and select Lists, then Create List. You can also collaborate with family and roommates to make sure you get everything your household needs. To invite someone, select the list you want to collaborate on, and click on the "+Invite" button. Alexa will provide a link which you can send to others, or it can send an email to them automatically.

Amazon Alexa – Smart home

There's no doubting that Alexa is the king of the smart home. Thanks to the easy-to-develop skills and popularity of the Echo devices, Alexa is the first stop for smart home manufacturers. Google Home is slowly starting to catch up, but Amazon maintains a strong lead. And, as new products are launched, most come with Alexa support, while Google Assistant support can be delayed, although this is starting to change.

Amazon's voice control is simple, although you need to format your phrase carefully. The phrasing changes from device to device. For most smart home devices you can say something along the lines of, "Alexa, turn on living room lights".

Other devices require you to ask the skill to do something. If you want to turn on your Dyson

360 Eye robot vacuum cleaner, for example, you have to say, "Alexa, ask Dyson to turn on". Remembering what your devices are called and which phrasing to use can be tricky at times. This isn't helped by Alexa occasionally mishearing what you're saying, performing an action on a different device entirely.

Thanks to more recent updates, Amazon Alexa now lets you sort devices into groups, and also lists devices by type. This makes finding the one you want much easier. And, you can control devices from the app, too, say setting the temperature on your Nest Thermostat or changing the colour of a Philips Hue bulb. It's still not perfect; you can't, at the time of writing, change the temperature of a Honeywell Evohome system.

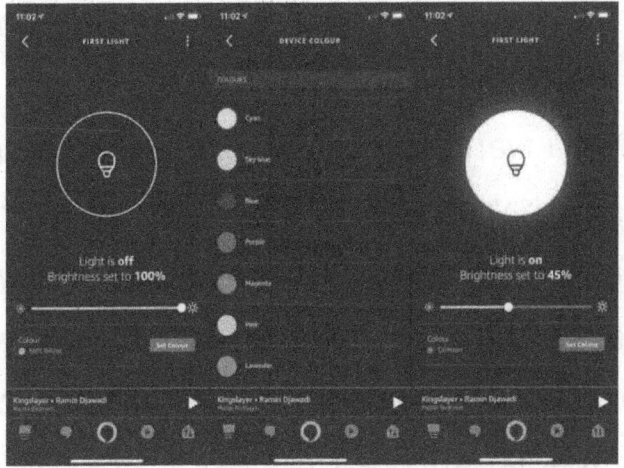

However, you can group multiple devices together for combined control, and you can change the name of a device in the app. As of a recent update, you can now include your Alexa devices in a smart home group. This makes the associated Alexa device 'aware' of where it's placed. For example, if you create a group for your living room and include all of your lights and an Alexa device, you can talk directly to that Echo and say, "Alexa, turn off lights". This will turn off all lights, without you having to mention which ones you want to turn off.

Likewise, you can set a temperature on your smart thermostat without having to say which device you want to control. It's a simple update, but one that makes Alexa far smarter than previously, and easier to control, shortening the commands that you have to use. If you want to control a device outside of that group, you can just name it, such as, "Alexa, turn off dining room light".

In-app, groups have a toggle on/off switch, so you can turn off compatible devices all in one go. Compatible devices are those that act like a switch, including smart plugs and smart lights.

Smartly, with some devices, Amazon pulls in the default sorting. For example, with Philips Hue bulbs Alexa can see and control the rooms that you've already configured. This is something that Google Home can't do.

Each smart home device can be disabled if you don't want voice control of it, but you can't remove devices from the app; this can only be done through the web portal.

More recently, Amazon has enabled Routines, letting you perform a few steps at once when you say a particular phrase. For example, you could set "Alexa, goodbye" to switch off all of your lights when you go out. Routines are currently very limited and let you turn lights on and off, and toggle some modes on some thermostats but not all. With Nest thermostats, you can't use Routines at all. Honeywell Evohome lets you trigger specific options, such as turning on Away mode.

Largely, the issue comes down to the way that the manufacturer created its Echo Skill. Those manufacturers that let their devices be individually grouped and enable special modes, such as Hue Scenes or Honeywell modes, to be seen in the app are generally the most flexible. The worst skills are those that require you to ask the Skill do to something, such as starting a clean. For these types of Skill, Alexa can't see the underlying hardware, so can't use these devices in Routines.

Brief mode is another great, recent addition. Rather than Alexa babbling away telling you what you've done, when you've just asked to turn a light down, Brief mode gets Alexa to respond to simple commands with a low beep. That makes the system far easier to use, still giving you a little bit of audible feedback that the command has been received.

Amazon Alexa – Music

Echo devices can play music from Sonos, TuneIn radio or, of course, Amazon Prime Music. You can even group multiple Echo devices to have music play through them all, although this feature doesn't support Spotify. And, creating a group has to be done in the app in a fairly clunky way; it certainly isn't as easy as grouping together your Sonos speakers.

Music quality depends on the device you're using. Voice control is neat, but it isn't always easy to say exactly what you want to listen to – I find that trying to specify a particular Spotify playlist often leads to the wrong track being played. It's far more effective to use the Spotify app to select the track or playlist you want and then use Spotify Connect to send the audio to an Echo. Voice commands work far better for pausing, skipping and changing volume.

Sonos integration is great to see, and you can do all of the same things to your players as you can Echo devices. The only restrictions are that you can't group or ungroup players, and you can't adjust the group volume on pre-grouped devices. Neatly, when you trigger Alexa the Sonos volume is dipped, so that your Echo can pick-up your command more easily.

However, it's frustrating that Alexa dips the volume of all Sonos players. It would be better if you could place devices into rooms; that way, when you triggered one Echo, it would only have to temporarily drop the volume of one device.

Commands are also quite clunky, and as mentioned above, recalling the exact phrasing to use can be a pain. For example, I found that "Alexa, stop playing in the office" didn't work; but, "Alexa, stop playing music in the office" did.

Again, it's just as hard to get Sonos to play the right track or playlist, so I prefer to set things off with the main Sonos app, using Alexa for volume, play/pause and volume control.

Amazon has also recently boosted the quality of the audio from its own Echo speakers. While the likes of the Amazon Echo Plus (2nd) gen are better to listen to than their predecessors, Amazon has now added the ability to create a stereo pair, so you can use two of the same Echo speakers together, one for the left channel and one for the right channel.

How to Connect a Nest Thermostat to Alexa

The Nest Learning Thermostat is already pretty good at knowing the temperature at which you're most comfortable, but if you want even more precise control, you can command it through Amazon's Alexa voice assistant. Using nothing but your voice, you can raise and lower the temperature, without leaving the comfort of your couch or bed. Here's how to link the Nest and Alexa.

1. Open the Amazon Alexa app, and select Devices. The Devices tab is the icon on the bottom right that's shaped like a home.

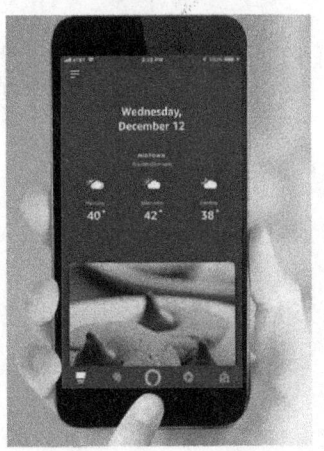

2. Press the plus sign in the top right corner.

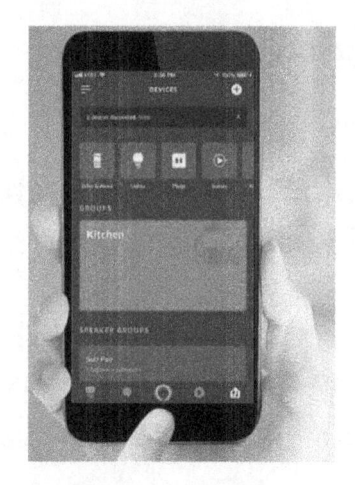

3. Select Add Device.

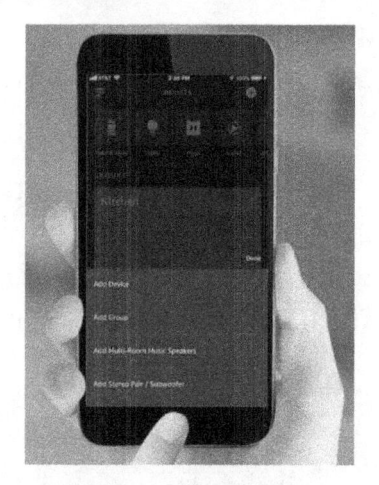

4. Select Thermostat.

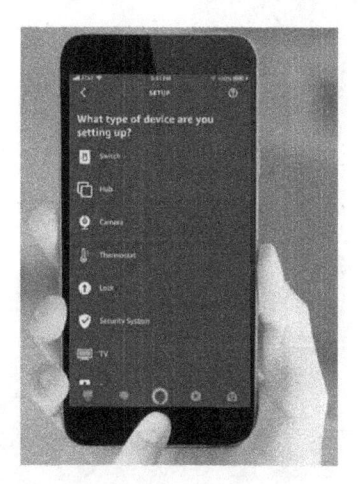

5. Select "Nest."

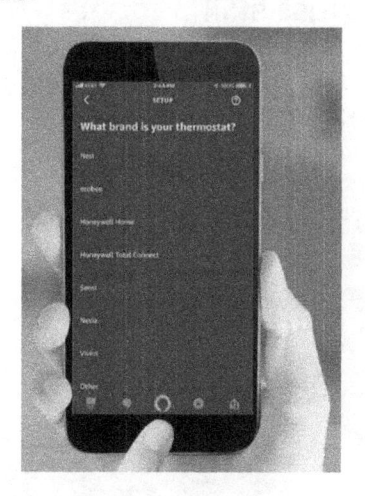

6. Download the Nest app.

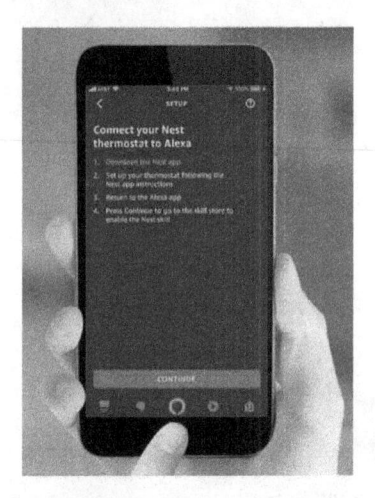

7. Enable the Nest skill.

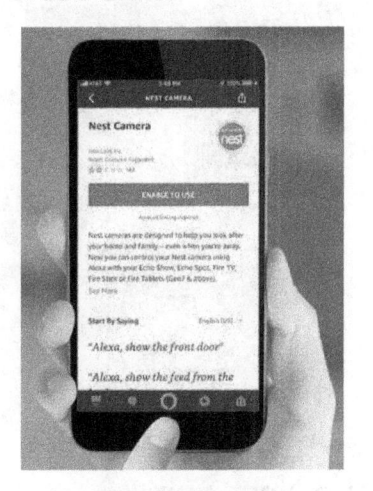

8. Log in to your Nest account.

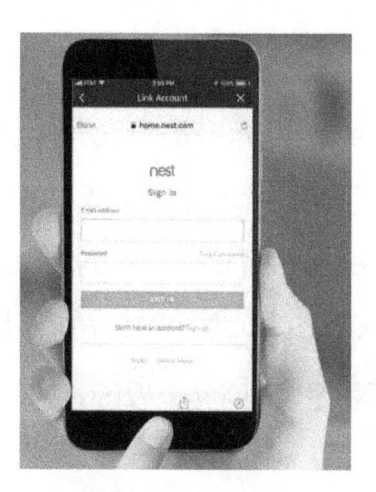

9. Press Discover Devices.

10. Select your Nest Thermostat.

You're all set. You can now say phrases such as "Alexa, change temperature to 75 degrees," or "Change Nest to 71 degrees" to set the temperature in your home.

How to Connect Philips Hue Lights to Amazon Echo

Connecting the Philips Hue lights to the Amazon Echo or Echo Dot—or any of Amazon's Alexa-enabled devices—is fairly easy, but if you want to do more than just dim and brighten your lights, it will take a few more steps. Here's how to do it.

1. Open the Alexa app, and select the Smart Home tab in the bottom right corner (the little house shape).

2. Select the plus sign in the top right corner.

3. Press the button on the Philips Hue bridge. Note: If you have an Echo Plus, you can skip this step, as the bulbs can connect directly to the

Plus. However, we recommend using the Hue bridge (and the Philips Hue app), as it allows for much greater control over the lights.

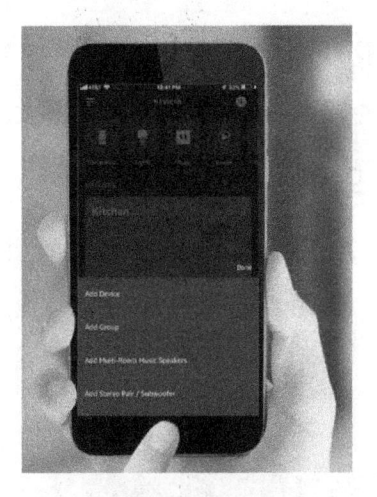

4. Select "Add Device." A screen will appear, saying Alexa is discovering devices; after, your Philips Hue bulbs should appear in the Devices section of the Alexa app.

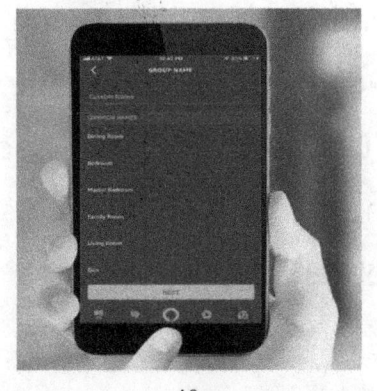

5. Group lights with other smart home devices. Under the Groups tab in the Alexa app, you can select multiple smart home devices so that you can control them as one. This is especially handy if you're grouping them by room. You can either add your Hue lights to an existing group, or create a new group.

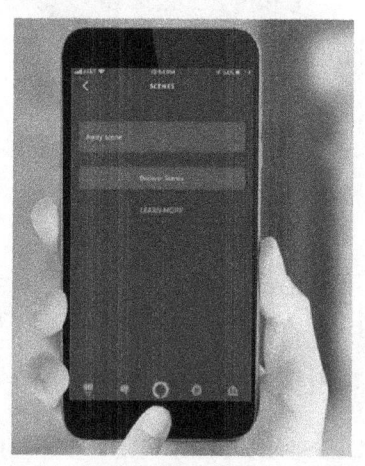

6. Control Philips Hue lighting scenes. If you've created a scene in the Philips Hue app, you can discover and control it through Alexa. Select the Scenes tab, "Discover Scenes," and scroll to the one you want. This tab also displays scenes created by other apps, such as the Logitech

Harmony remotes, so it can get confusing as to what scene you want to activate.

How to Change the Color of Your Philips Hue Lights Using Alexa

If you have Philips Hue lights that can change color, you can control what color they change to from within the Alexa app.

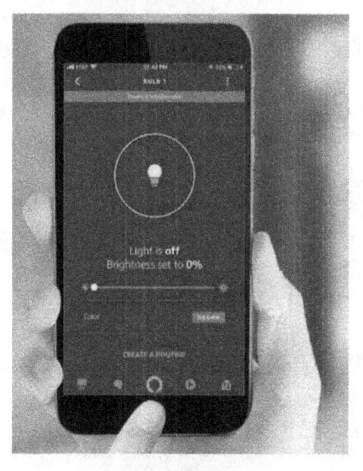

1. From the Devices menu, select the light whose color you wish to change. Here, you can also turn the light on and off, adjust its brightness, and change its name.

2. Press the Set Color button at the bottom.

3. Select the color you want. Note that the Alexa app limits you to 16 colors; if you are looking for more options, you can verbally say one of the hundreds of colors that work with Alexa, use the Philips Hue app itself, or set up a custom command using IFTTT.

How to Connect an Amazon Echo to a Harmony Remote

The Logitech Harmony Elite universal remote control, as well as other Harmony remotes, can control a range of smart home devices. For instance, you can connect your TV to your Apple

TV and your stereo for the ultimate home theater. You can also link the commands and activities you create for the remote to your Amazon Echo.

Bear in mind that the only things you'll be able to control using Alexa are activities you've already created on the Harmony remote, so make sure you've completed that step before connecting it to the Amazon Echo.

1. Open the Alexa app, and select Skills & Games from the Home menu (press the three horizontal buttons on the top left).

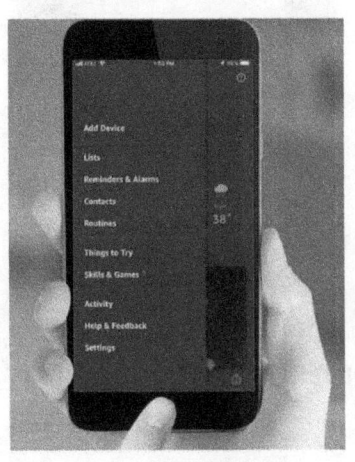

2. Search for "Harmony" and select the result with the blue Harmony logo.

3. Enable the Harmony skill.

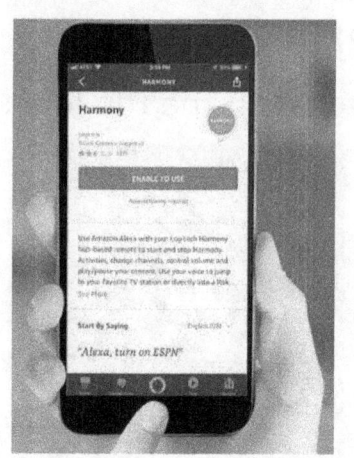

4. Login to your Logitech Harmony account.

5. Select the activities you wish to control using Alexa. You can also choose the wording to activate a particular activity.

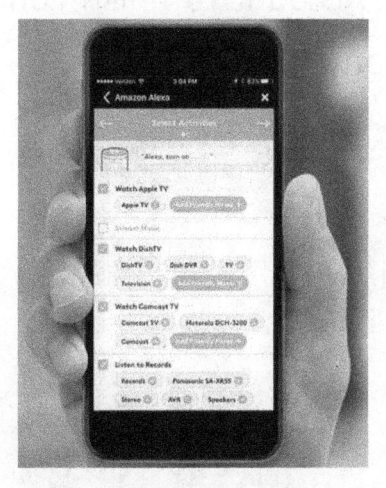

7. Select the TV stations you wish to control using Alexa. This way, you can simply say

"Alexa, turn on ESPN," and it will automatically change the channel for you.

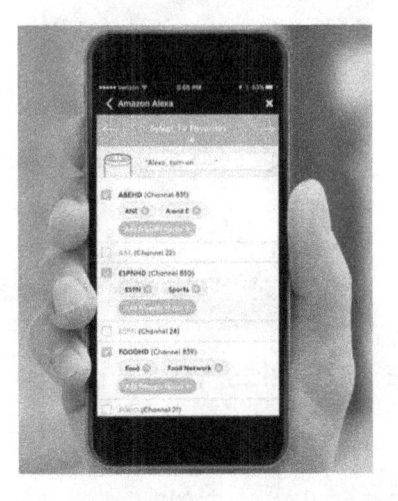

8. Press Link Account to finish connecting Alexa to your Harmony remote.

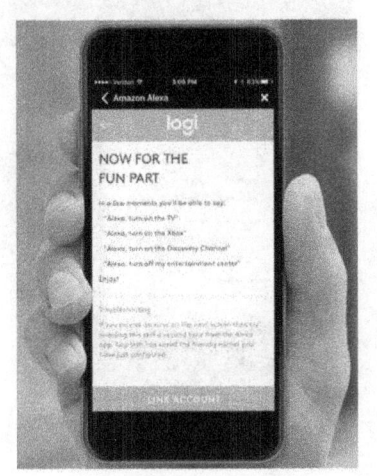

How to create an Amazon Echo stereo pair

Stereo pairing is a trick used by many manufacturers, letting you use two wireless speakers, one for the left channel and one for the right channel. With the Google Home Max, Apple HomePod and a range of Sonos speakers, such as the Sonos One, supporting stereo pairing, it was only a matter of time before Amazon got in on the act. Here's how to create an Amazon Echo stereo pair.

Before you start, it's essential that you have two of the same type of speaker. You can't mix and match your models or generations of speakers. For the latest generation that's two Echo Dot (3rd Gen), two Echo or two Echo Plus (2nd Gen) speakers that you'll need. The original Echo Plus is supported, but older products aren't. Once you've got two connected to your account, here's what you need to do.

1. Start the stereo pairing mode

Open the Amazon Alexa app and tap the control icon at the bottom right of the screen, then select one of the Amazon Echo speakers that you want to control. In the Connected Devices section you'll see Stereo Pair / Subwoofer, so select this option. Read the next page of advice and, when ready, tap Next to continue.

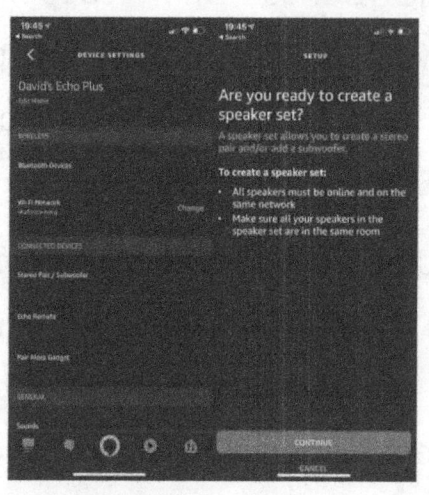

2. Choose your speakers

Next, select two speakers of the same type from the list of your Amazon Echo devices. Once you choose the first one, the only choices not greyed out will be the speakers that you can choose. Tap the next button.

You'll see the name of one of the speakers at the top of the app, and a choice 'Left' or 'Right'. Annoyingly, Amazon can't play a sound out of the selected speaker to help you identify it, so you may have to guess (don't worry you can flip the choice later).

Once you've chosen, tap Next and the Amazon Alexa app will assign the channel you didn't choose to the other Echo speaker.

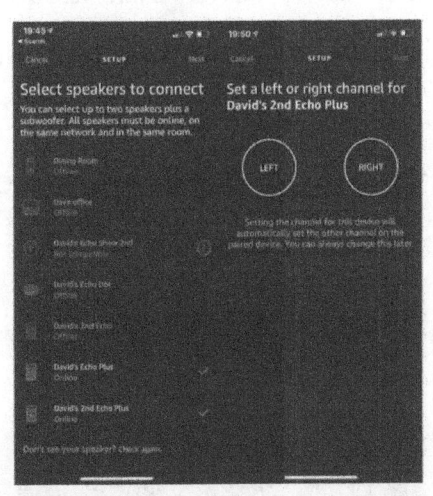

3. Finish the job

You'll see a progress bar as Alexa connects your two speakers. When done you'll get a new Stereo Pair listed, with the names of the two speakers that you used. Tap either speaker and you can choose which channel it is: left or right.

To get back to this screen, tap the Control icon in the Alexa app and you'll see your Stereo Pair listed under Speaker Groups. You can use the Delete Speaker Set option to split your two Echo devices apart.

When in a stereo pair, music will come out of both speakers, only one will act as the left channel and one the right channel. Volume control applies to both speakers. If you ask Alexa a question, just the speaker closest to you in the stereo pair will reply.

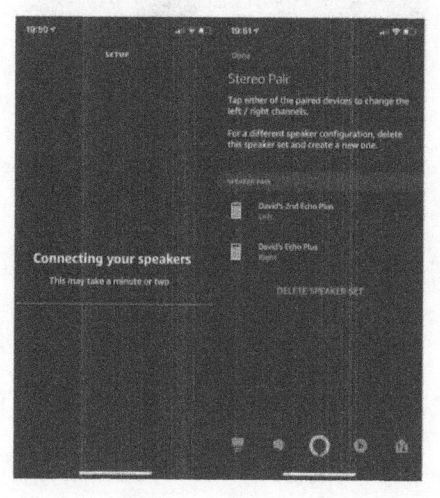

How to add an Amazon Echo Sub and configure Alexa EQ settings

The Amazon Echo Sub is a standalone product that adds extra bass to an existing Echo speaker. In this guide, we'll show you how to add an Amazon Echo Sub and configure Alexa EQ settings, so you can get the most out of the bass speaker.

You add an Echo Sub in the same way as any speaker. When you first add the speaker, Alexa will take you through the pairing process with another Echo Speaker (or two for a stereo pair). If you've already created a stereo pair, you first have to delete that pair. We'll show you how to add the Sub manually.

Finally, you need a supported Echo device. The current list of supported devices includes the Amazon Echo (1st Gen), Amazon Echo (2nd Gen), Echo Dot (3rd Gen), Echo Plus (1st Gen), Echo Plus (2nd Gen), Echo Show (1st Gen) and

Echo Show (2nd Gen). Only the Echo (2nd Gen), Echo Dot (3rd Gen) and either generation Echo Plus can be used as a stereo pair with the Sub.

Step 1 – Create a speaker group with the sub

Open the Alexa app and tap the control icon at the bottom right of the screen. Tap the Plus icon and, from the menu that appears, pick the Add Stereo Pair / Subwoofer option. Read the instructions to make sure your speakers are in the right state for pairing and then tap Continue.

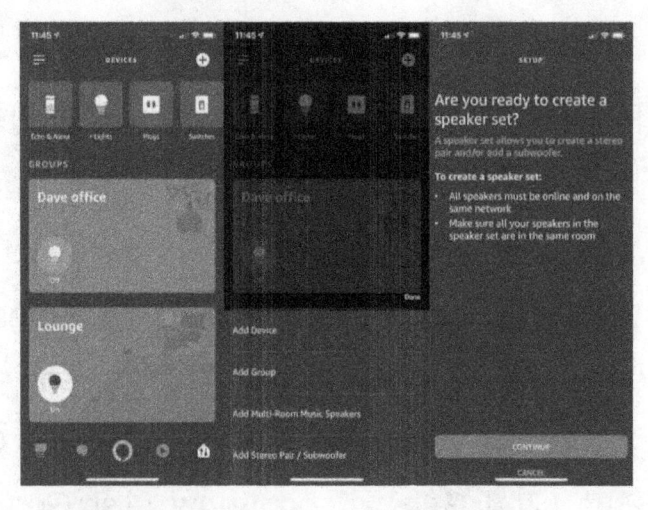

Step 2 – Select the speakers to use

From the list of your Echo speakers, tap the Echo Sub first. This will change the list above, so that you can only select the speakers that are compatible with the Sub. You can select one or two speakers from the list. The latter creates a stereo pair and only works if you select two speakers of the same type from this list. When done tap Next and the speaker group will be created.

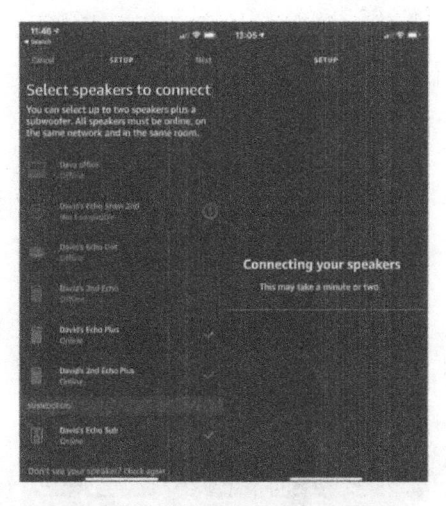

Step 3 – Manage Alexa EQ settings

You can adjust the sound of your speakers using the EQ settings. Go to the Alexa app and tap the control icon (bottom right). Then tap Echo &

Alexa and select one of the Echo speakers that's in a speaker group with the Sub; note you can't get to the EQ if you pick the Sub.

Tap Sound under General and then select Equalizer under Media. You can use the sliders to increase or decrease the Bass, Midrange or Treble. Tap the back arrow when you're done. Note that EQ changes apply to all speakers in a group.

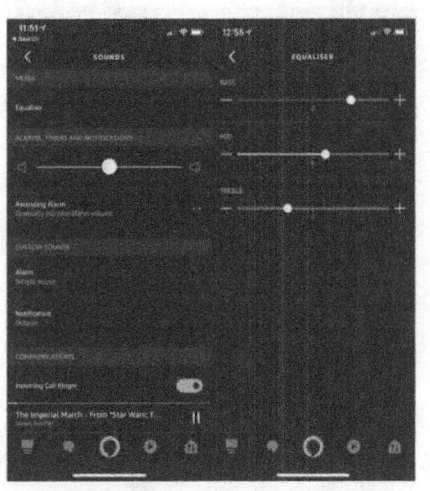

Step 4 – Delete the Sub pairing

If you want to attach the Echo Sub to a different product, you have to delete the pairing first. Go to the Alexa app and tap the control icon (bottom right) and select your speaker group from the bottom of the page. Tap Delete Speaker Set and you're done.

Alexa Tips & Tricks

Add Skills

Out of the box, your smart speaker can do loads but it can't do everything. That's where Skills come in. These expand Alexa's capabilities and can do everything from reading you a customised bedtime story to giving you control of a smart thermostat.

To add a Skill go to the app and tap the menu button, then select Skills & Games. You can browse by top picks and categories or use the Search facility to find a particular Skill. Tap Your Skills and you can see and manage the ones that you already have installed.

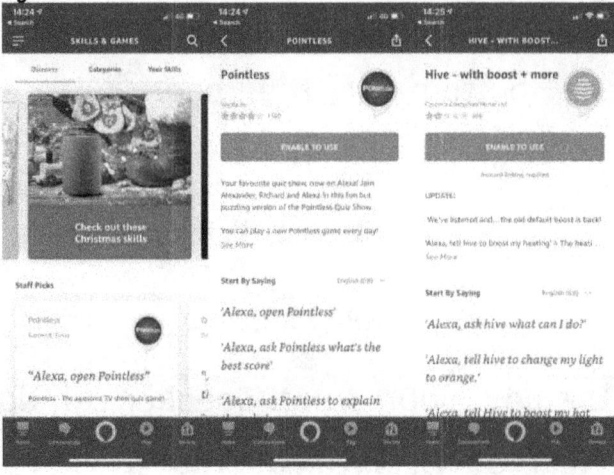

Group devices together

To make your smart home easier to use, you can group smart devices into rooms alongside an Echo device. Once you do this, saying, "Alexa, turn on the light", for example, will turn on the light(s) in the same room as your Echo speaker. That's far easier than having to specify which lights you want.

Add routines

If you want Alexa to do more than one thing at once, you need Alexa Routines. With one command, you can tell Alexa to turn off your lights, turn up the heating and give you a news flash, for example. It's easy to create simple routines to do everything you want.

Change your default music service

Don't want music to come from Amazon Music? No worries, as you can change the default music streaming service to Spotify and, soon, Apple Music. Go to Settings in the Alexa app and tap Music. You'll need to select Spotify to sign into your account, then you can use the Choose default music services to select this as your main music service. Next time you ask Alexa to play a song, it will come from your Spotify account.

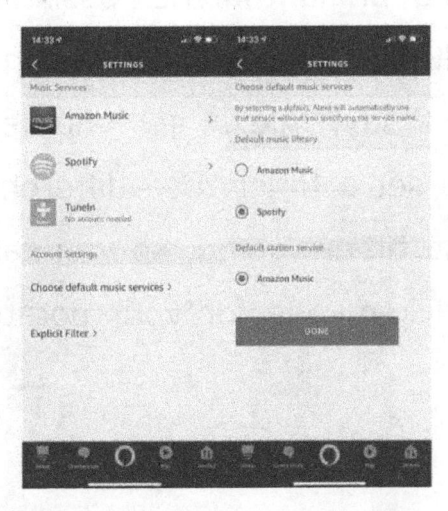

Boost your music with two speakers (and a Sub)

Why stand for just one speaker when you can use two of the same type of Echo together in a stereo pair. In this kind of mode, one acts as the left channel and one as the right channel. Find out how to create an Amazon Echo stereo pair.

If you want to take things further, you can add an Echo Sub into the mix to give you that extra low-frequency push. Find out how to add an Amazon Echo sub.

Set multiple timers

The Echo is a brilliant kitchen assistant, and can handle multiple timers, which is brilliant when cooking. Just say, "Alexa, set <name> timer, xx minutes" to set a timer. Use different names to get different timers going, so you can have one for your chicken, one for your potatoes and so on.

If you've got an Amazon Echo show, you can see the timers on-screen; speaker-only Echo devices will read out which timer has finished.

Change the wake word

If you live with someone called Alexa (or even Alex), you probably find that your Echo devices go off all of the time. Fortunately, you can change the wake word to prevent this from happening.

Go to the Alexa app and select Devices. Tap Echo & Alexa and then pick the Echo device that you want to change. Tap Wake word and then choose the word you want to use to wake your Echo up: Alexa, Amazon, Echo or Computer.

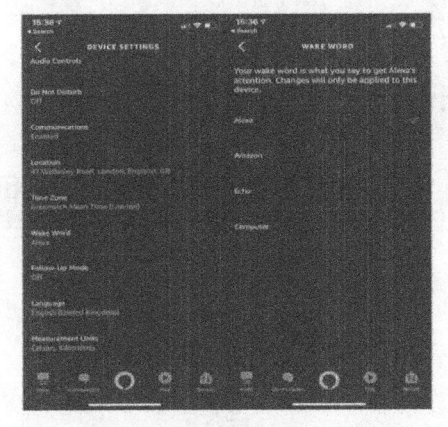

Make Alexa less annoying

By default, Alexa tells you everything that it's done, but you can make her quieter if you don't want to get a deluge of speech when you turn on a light. You can fix this with Brief Mode. Open the Alexa app and go to Settings, then tap Alexa Account.

Tap Alexa Voice Responses and you can turn Brief Mode on. Now, when you ask Alexa to do a lot of things, such as turning on a light, she'll respond with a beep rather than a sentence.

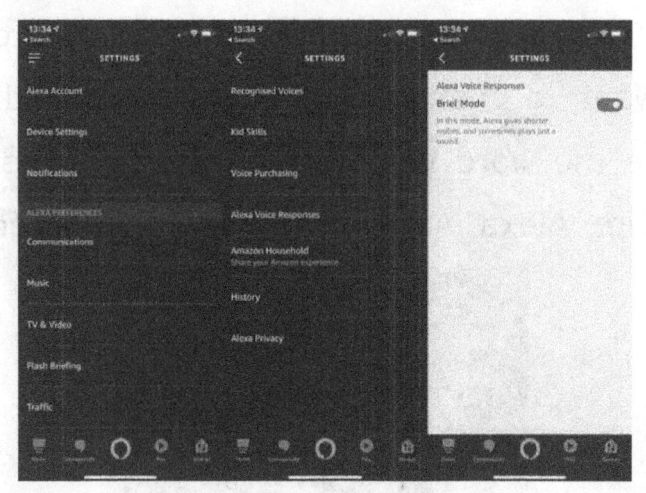

Set an alarm

Who needs an alarm clock when you have an Echo? Just say, "Alexa, set alarm <time>" and you'll get your alarm the next day. You can say, "Alexa, snooze" to get a few more minutes in bed or "Alexa, stop" to turn the alarm off.

Get things done one after the other with Follow-Up mode

With Follow-Up mode, your Echo will keep listening after completing a task, so you can ask Alexa to do something else. This is handy if you, say, want to turn on light down and then turn the heating up.

Follow-Up mode has to be enabled on a per-device basis. Go to Settings in the Alexa app and select Device. Tap Echo & Alexa, then select the Echo speaker that you want to change. Tap Follow-Up Mode and turn the setting on.

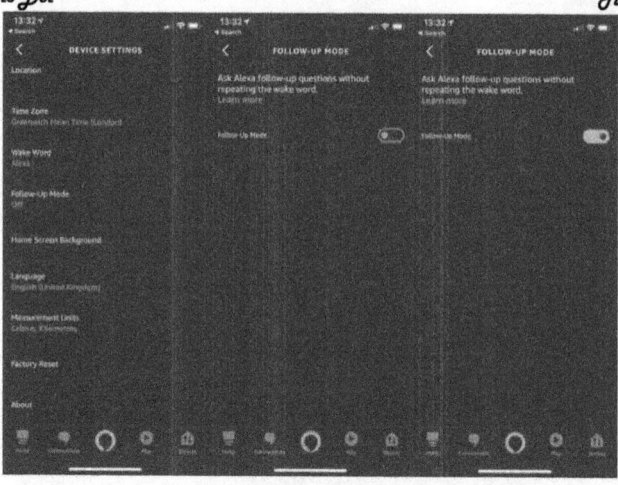

Enable Night Light

Night Light

labworks.io ltd
★★★½☆ 339

ENABLE TO USE

BEFORE ENABLING THIS SKILL PLEASE READ THE FAQs

"Undoubtably the best night light skill in the Alexa store" - Chuck Norris (probably)....
See More

Start By Saying   English (US) ∨

"Alexa, open Night Light"

The light ring on the top of the Echo device may be used as a night light. Go to the Skills & Games section on the left menu in the Alexa app. Type night light in the search bar. Find the night light skill by labworks.io Ltd and tap ENABLE TO USE.

Once the skill is enabled, activate the night light by saying "Alexa, open night light" and state how long you want the night light on. For example "Alexa, open night light for 45 minutes."

Add Email & Calendar

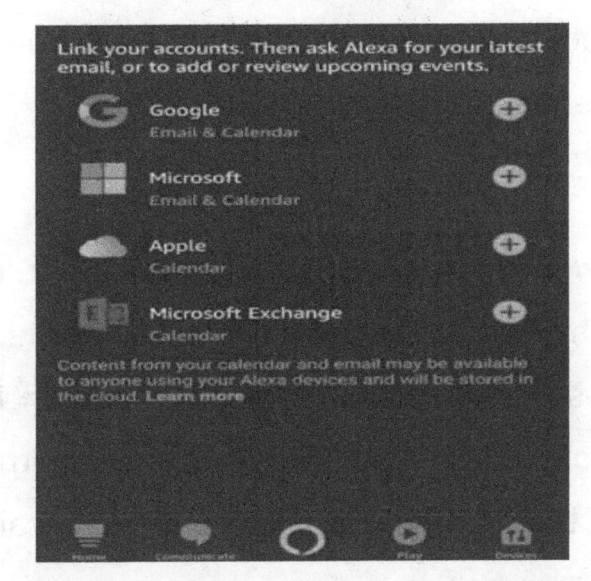

Having Alexa access your calendars and email can be very useful if you want her to read your email to you or add an event to your calendar.

To link your calendar and email to your Alexa, go to the left menu by tapping the 3 lines in the upper left corner. Once in the menu, tap Settings, scroll down and tap Email & Calendar.

You can choose from connecting your Google email and calendar, Microsoft email and calendar, Apple calendar, and Microsoft Exchange calendar. Choose which one you'd like to connect. If you pick Google or Microsoft you can choose whether to connect both your email and calendar.

Create multiple profiles

Alexa will listen to anyone – but that doesn't mean she has to treat everyone the same. If you set up separate profiles for each person in your household, you can switch between them to ensure that any music played, calendars accessed, and accounts used for shopping will be appropriate to that particular user.

Creating a new profile has to be done by the registered owner of the Echo device. Open Settings in the Alexa app, click Household Profile in the Settings section and then enter your account password. Now get the other member to log in using the same device and link your accounts.

A word of warning: when you tell Alexa to order an item from Amazon, the system will use whichever payment method is set up for the active profile – so to avoid mix-ups, it's worth checking before you place the order. To do so, just ask "Alexa, which profile is this?"

Protect your purchases

On the subject of voice purchases, if you've got kids in the house you'll probably want to set up a PIN code for online shopping, to ensure they don't order a new LEGO kit every two weeks. To do this, scroll down to Voice Purchasing in the Alexa app and add the code in the "Require voice code" field. This will need to be spoken when making a purchase – so make sure they don't overhear you.

Use IFTTT

You probably already know about the free-to-use automation service IFTTT – the web service is now used by supermarkets among other parties. For home use, though, what's perhaps more handy is the numerous Alexa integrations the service now offers.

To get started, go to ifttt.com/amazon_alexa and click Connect. Enter your password on the Amazon page that appears and authorise the connection. You can now use the pre-rolled applets to link Alexa to a huge range of services and devices – from a Roomba vacuum cleaner or a WeMo coffee maker to Facebook Messenger and Google spreadsheets.

In our view, one of the most useful integrations is between Alexa and task management app Wunderlist: although Alexa already has a native shopping-list feature, Wunderlist is more flexible and works across almost every platform imaginable.

To set it up, search IFTTT for "wunderlist" and you should see a result entitled "Add Amazon Echo shopping list items to Wunderlist". Click the Turn On toggle switch, and on the next screen enter "me@wunderlist.com" in the "To:" field, before clicking Save.

Now open IFTTT's settings (by clicking your name at the top of the IFTTT interface) and link your Google account. If you have more than one Google account, make a note of the one you used.

Finally, sign in to Wunderlist and open your account settings, again by clicking your name at the top of the sidebar. Click "Add or manage your email addresses", and make sure that the email address you just linked to IFTTT is allowed to add items to your list by email. Now, when you tell Alexa to add something to your shopping list, it will be forwarded onto Wunderlist, ready for you to pick up on the web or on your phone.

Personalise your Flash Briefing

A Flash Briefing is Amazon's name for a quick info dump that draws content from multiple sources, such as news publishers, weather forecasters and exchange rate trackers. To set one up that's personalised just for you, open the Alexa app and click Flash Briefing in the Settings section. Click "Get more Flash Briefing content" and select the elements you would like to add: you will find options such as BBC World Service, The Guardian, MTV and the Joke of the Day.

Each one you add will be automatically enabled, but you can remove any source from the briefing if you choose: just return to the Flash Briefing section and toggle the switch beside each one's name.

You can enable sports content within the Flash Briefing, too – but Alexa already knows a lot about football and other sports. Click Sports Update on the Settings screen, then use the search box to find the teams you're interested in. As well as the huge Premier League clubs, you will also find local teams such as Leatherhead and Taunton Town – although, tragically, Lewes FC is missing from the list.

Say goodbye, Alexa

If you're upgrading from a Dot to a Plus, or from a regular Alexa to a Show, you might be tempted to pass your old device on to a friend, or sell it online. Before you do, make sure you deregister it so that the new owner can't place online orders using your account. Open the Alexa app, click Settings, then click on the name of the device you're getting rid of. You will find the deregistration option in the About section.

Don't worry about the record that Alexa keeps of things you've said to her: this won't follow the device to its new home. However, if you ever want to purge this information from your own account, you can delete individual recordings from the homepage of the Alexa app, or switch to your Amazon account to delete the lot.

To do this, log in at amazon.co.com, click Your Account, and find the link to "Manage Your Content and Devices". Switch to the Your Devices tab, click the three dots beside the names of each of your Echo speakers, and choose "Manage voice recordings" on each one. Read the disclaimer and click Delete to wipe the slate clean.

Top essential Alexa Skills to try first

Having tried and tested some of the most popular Alexa skills, here are the ones you'll want to get right away, a handful of niceties worth checking out, and some you'll want to avoid for now.

1. Roomba: Control your robot vac

iRobot's Roomba robot vacs are some of the best around, and now they'll digest your voice commands as well as gobbling up stray pet hairs.

Well, if you have one of the fancier web connected Roomba models, such as the 900 Series – and live in the US – that is.

The latest major update to the iRobot HOME App for Android and iOS introduces the skill, so all you need to do is say, "Alexa, tell Roomba to start cleaning," and you can kick back with your beverage of choice.

It's frustrating that it's currently limited to the States, of course, but no one said living the smart home dream was going to be easy.

2. Skill Finder: Find more skills!

Amazon has introduced a neat Alexa skill that will helps you find more Alexa skills.

It's a quick and easy way to discover cool new integrations you might not know about, simply by asking things like, "Alexa, tell Skill Finder to give me the Skill of the Day".

Alternatively, it'll let you unearth skills on a category-by-category basis, so query, "Alexa, tell Skill Finder to list the top skills in the games category," and you'll be served up the most popular gaming-related integrations.

3. Plex: Manage your media

This is probably our new favourite Alexa skill as it lets you control your media library without lifting a finger.

If you use Plex Media Server and have an Echo device in your living room, you can now ask Alexa to play films, tell you what's next on your Plex deck, and even suggest things you might want to want.

"Alexa, play the next episode of Prison Break but don't tell my boss!"

4. TrackR: Find your phone

If you sign up for a TrackR account, you can shout 'Alexa, find my phone' and your handset will immediately ring at full volume. It's properly useful for forgetful people and works a treat.

5. Hive: Control your heating

The Hive skill lets you control the temperature of your house using Alexa – and there's a bit of banter for good measure.

If you turn the heating off when your house is warm, Alexa might comment; and by comment, we mean she'll say something that comes off as slightly sarcastic.

Still, it saves you the effort of actually having to get up to adjust the temperature.

6. Hue: Control your lights

Your Echo assistant has known how to play nice with Hue lights for a while, but these days you have more mood control options than ever.

Want to make things all sexy? Set up a 'romantic' profile and Alexa will make your bedroom redder than downtown Amsterdam before you can so much as say, "Giggity."

7. Control your thermostat

Alexa now supports the Nest range of Learning Thermostats, meaning you can simply say "Hey Alexa, raise the living room temperature by 2 degrees," and you'll be toastier than chestnuts roasting on an open fire.

8. Uber: Call for a ride

Uber is a little fiddly to set up with Alexa, but once you've got it sorted, it does feel a little bit like magic.

It took us a couple of attempts to link an Uber account to our Echo, and If you try to just ask for an Uber, Alexa will tell you to ask for it in a specific way.

After you've got the knack though, just say the necessary incantation and a ride will roll up outside your location. Neat.

9. 7-Minute Workout: Get a guide workout

Just say, "Alexa, start 7-minute workout," and shock of all horrors, Alexa will take your candy ass through a 7-minute workout!

If you're unsure of any of the exercises, the app on your phone will show you little pictures of what you should do.

It'd be nice if Alexa was a bit more encouraging, or played some music to help motivate you, but it's pretty good all the same.

10. Spotify: The best for music streaming

Spotify is the best music streaming service around, and with Echo, Premium subscribers can simply shout out what they want to be played, be it a specific artist, mood, playlist and even decade.

It's a no-brainer to enable as soon as you fire up your new smart speaker and, better still, it comes pre-loaded – just enable it as your default music player and you're away.

11. Wake up to your favourite song

While we're on the subject of music, as of December 18, Echo users can now command Alexa to wake them up to the tunes of their choice. Whether you need some heavy metal to stun you out of your slumber, or some Marvin Gaye for a relaxing Sunday morning in bed with the paper, Alexa has you covered.

You won't need an additional Skill download for this; just say "Alexa wake me at 8am to..." and choose from artists, playlists, tracks or even a random selection. Best news is it works with all supported music services.

12. Control your whole home entertainment set-up

If you're the proud owner of a Logitech Harmony Hub and a compatible remote, then you can use your Echo to add voice controls. You can command Alexa to turn on the TV or media player, or play and pause content on your television screen, This is particularly handy if you've lost the remote down the back of the sofa.

A recent improvement even simplified the voice controls. You can simply say "Alexa, turn up the volume/turn on BBC 1."

13. The Guardian: All the latest news

Ask Alexa for the latest news, headlines, podcasts and more with this skill – she'll even read your entire articles if you want.

It's well useful for all those times you want to meditate on how horrible the world is whilst doing the washing up.

14. Sky Sports: Never miss a goal

Getting mad when your team concedes a last minute equalizer has never been easier, as Alexa will feed you back all the latest scores and sport news.

It's available on your snazzzy right out of the box, so all you have to do is ask.

15. National Rail: Get train updates

Gone are the days of having to fiddle with an app to find out Southern's fecked up your commute again.

With Echo, all you'll need to do is chat to Alexa for a breakdown of the latest morning misery. Crying into your porridge? That bit will likely remain a constant.

16. Google Calendar: Never miss a meeting again

Habitually late to – or forget – pretty much everything? Alexa might just be your saviour, as you can ask your Echo to remind you about meetings and other important events

Neglected an anniversary, for example? Combine your reminder with begging Alexa to order some last minute flowers for the ultimate in time-efficient getting out of jail.

17. Control Fire TV with your Echo

Most Amazon Fire TV devices now come with an Alexa voice remote, but if it's across the other side of the room, that's a whole lot of energy expenditure that could be used for keeping warm. So, US Echo owners (and we're hoping UK soon), can now control their Fire TV devices with Alexa on the Amazon Echo.

You could say "Alexa open Hulu" or Alexa "show me comedy films" for example. You can even say "Show me films with Clint Eastwood," leveraging the universal search feature.

If you only have one Fire TV, Alexa should complete the pairing process automatically.

How to set up and use Alexa smart home groups

One of the main problems with a house stuffed full of smart home kit is having to try and remember what you've called everything: was it the lounge light or the living room light that you wanted to turn on? Now, with Alexa's improved smart home groups, that pain goes away. I'll show you how to set up and use Alexa smart home groups.

Groups have been available for a while but Amazon has dramatically improved them. Now, you can group your Echo devices with your smart home devices, which tells Alexa where it's located. That makes control far easier. For example, once you've grouped items together, you can just say, "Alexa, turn on the light", and your Echo understands which light your talking about with no further clarification. And, an update to the Sonos skill means that when you now talk to Alexa, on the Sonos player in the same room ducks its volume rather than your entire system.

Groups make it easier to understand and manage your home, too, as you place everything in one room together. In short, if you've got more than one Echo device, you'll want to follow these instructions. Please note, that not all third-party Amazon Alexa devices can be put into groups. For example, if you buy the Netgear Orbi Voice, it won't let you place it in a group. Using third-party devices often means going back to the older form of control where you tell Alexa which device you want to control.

1. Create a smart home group

Open the Alexa app and tap the Devices icon at the bottom-right of the screen. This will take you to the main smart home screen, listing all of your devices plus any groups that you might have. To add a new group tap the Plus icon and select Add group. You'll be given a list of common room names that you can choose from, although you can type in a custom name if you prefer. Tap Next when you're done.

Next, on the Define Group page you'll be given a list of smart devices that you can add. Choose the devices that are in this room, including any Amazon Echo devices, Sonos speakers, smart lights and even thermostats. Don't worry if you miss anything, as you can edit a Group later and add or remove devices. Tap Save when you're done.

2. Control your devices with the app

Back on the Devices page, you'll see your new group. Tap a group and you'll see all of your devices in there; you can tap Edit to make changes to the devices.

At the top of a group's page are All On and All Off buttons. Tap these to turn your group devices on or off. Note that this feature only works on devices that have switch-like capabilities, such as smart plugs and smart lights.

3. Control your devices with your voice

When you talk to an Echo that's in a group, you can use simplified commands to control smart devices. Here are a few to get you started:

"Alexa, turn on lights."

"Alexa, turn off lights."

"Alexa, set temperature to 19 degrees."

"Alexa, what is the thermostat temperature?"

This type of command is far easier than remembering device or group names. To control other devices from your grouped Echo, you can use the old style of command, naming the smart home device that you want to control, such as "Alexa, turn on office light."

4. Edit Alexa smart home device groups

Once you have created an Alexa smart home group you can change its settings and rename it. To do this just go to the Smart Home menu in the Alexa app, select Groups and choose the group you want to edit.

You can change the group name by selecting Edit Name, add or remove devices from the group or delete the group entirely by hitting the trash icon.

How to make Alexa Routines – smart home automation made easy

One of the best updates to the Echo family is Alexa Routines, enabling you to control multiple devices and perform multiple actions via a single phrase, such as "Alexa, goodbye". No longer do you have to reel off a long list of instructions – through simple automation, you can control devices faster.

Whether you want to turn off everything as you leave your home, or set your home up perfectly for a movie night, we'll show you how to build your own Routines. Since Alexa works in the cloud, these instructions apply for all devices, including the Echo, Echo Spot, Echo Show and Echo Dot.

Before you start, you'll need to have added any smart home devices that you want to control to your Amazon Alexa account.

1. Create a new Routine

Launch the Amazon Alexa app on your phone, tap the hamburger and select Routines. You'll see that there's a pre-made "Alexa, start my day" routine in there; we'll skip this for now, so tap the Create Routine button.

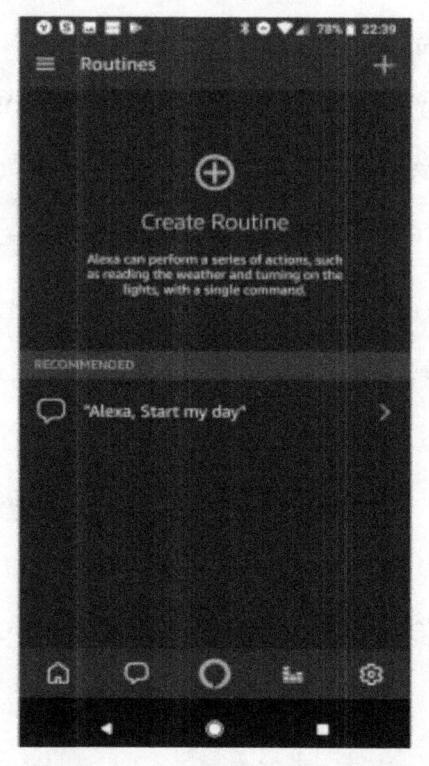

2. Create the start action

Routines can be triggered by a phrase, or set to turn on at a specific time (repeat options for multiple days are available). We'll start with a phrase, so tap "When you say something". Enter the word or phrase that you want to use: I've gone for "Alexa, Goodbye", so I can trigger the routine when I go out. Tap Save when you're done.

3. Choose your smart home actions

Tap Add action, then choose Smart Home. You can now choose to Control device or Control scene. Scenes are discovered by Alexa for certain products, such as a specific Philips Hue lighting mode.

Select Control device, and you'll see a list of your smart home devices. Currently, Alexa Routines can only control devices that have an on/off mode, or a brightness slider. This means you can't control a thermostat's temperature, for example.

Exact control differs from device to device. For example, with the Honeywell Evohome smart heating system, you can trigger modes such as Away, which sets every zone to 15ºC by default.

When selected most devices give you the option to turn them on or off; smart lighting options give you a brightness slider if you select to turn them off.

Select the option you want for the device you've selected and tap Next, and then tap Add. Repeat this step for any other smart home devices you want to control.

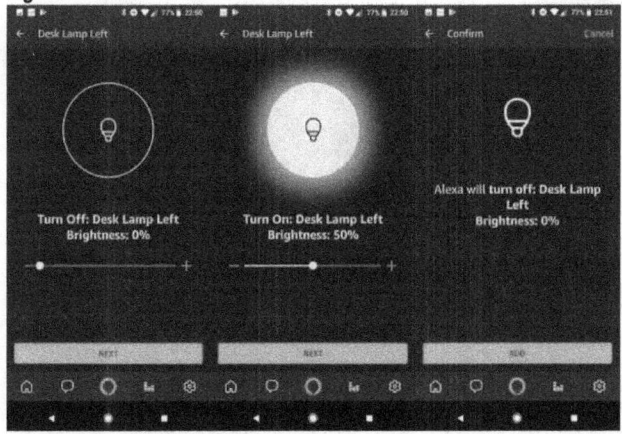

4. Choose other actions

As well as controlling smart home devices, Routines can also do other things: News reads out your Flash Briefing; Traffic gives you an update between the addresses set in your Alexa account; Weather gives you a local weather update; and Alexa Says lets you choose what Alexa will say when the Routine runs, choosing from a list of canned responses. Add as many other actions as you want.

5. Select the responding device

If you choose any option that requires Alexa to speak, such as a weather report, you can use the From option to pick which device will be used for the audio. You can force Alexa to speak from a set Echo, but the default option of "The device you speak to" is probably best, so Alexa will respond from which ever Echo you activated.

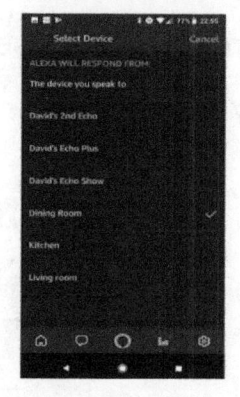

6. Create and run your routine

Tap the Create button and your Routine will be created. As the message says, it can take up to one minute for routines to be created and available. If you picked a time-based trigger, your routine will be activated automatically. Otherwise, you can just say your phrase, such as "Alexa, goodbye".

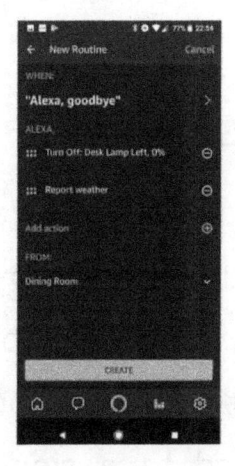

How to make Skype calls with Amazon Alexa

Amazon Echo devices already let you make voice and video calls between each other for free. As of a more recent update, you can now extend the capability and make Skype calls, too.

As well as making standard VoIP calls, you can use Skype to call landline numbers, and you get 200 free minutes to use. This puts Alexa closer to Google Assistant, which already gives you free landline calls. Incoming calls can also be answered from your Echo devices.

Getting it all working requires a bit of configuration, but we'll take you through the exact steps here.

Step 1 – Add the Skype Skill

Fire up the Amazon Alexa app and tap the menu button. Select Settings and tap Communications. Currently, there's only one option: Skype. Tap the Plus icon next to Skype and choose Sign In. You'll be redirected to a sign-in page, so just enter your Skype username and password when prompted.

Once signed in, you'll get a page showing all the things that Alexa will be able to do with your Skype account. Tap Yes to continue.

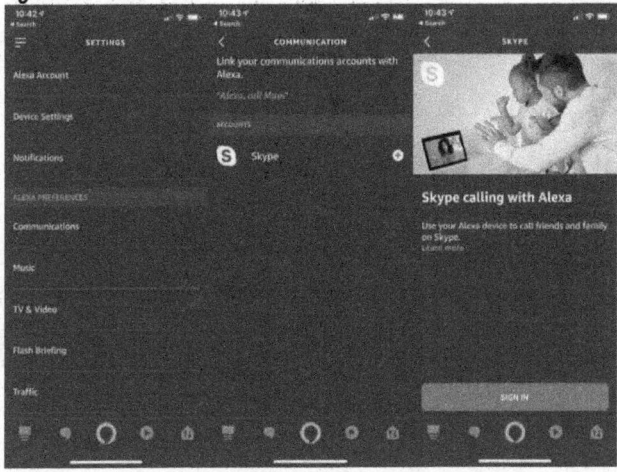

Step 2 – Confirm your settings

Once complete, you'll get a message telling you that your Skype is linked. Tap Done to confirm the changes. You'll then see the screen that shows you that your Skype account is linked to Alexa. If you change your mind, you can tap the Unlink account button.

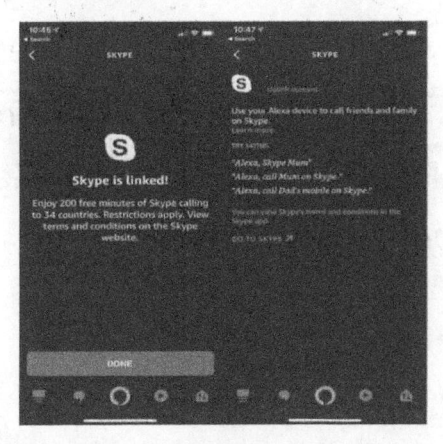

Step 3 – Make a call

Just say, "Alexa, Skype <name of contact>" and the call will be made. The Skype skill will pull contacts from your Skype account; if you install the mobile version, you can synchronise the contacts from your phone with your account to make things easy.

If you want to call a number that's not in your address book, you can just ask Alexa to call it (say the actual number) instead. Please note that the Skill can't look up local business addresses, which is a limitation compared to the Google Assistant skill.

All calls made go out without a Caller ID. If you have a Skype phone number, then calls are made with this. You can't synchronise your phone's Caller ID as you can with Google Home calling, though.

Step 4 – Answer a call

Incoming Skype calls will ring your Echo devices. To answer, just say, "Alexa, pick up". You'll then be connected to your call. You can say, "Alexa, hang up" to put down any call.

Amazon Alexa – Drop in, calls and messages

Amazon recently added voice and video calls, and the drop-in intercom feature. Both work either locally inside your home, or externally to friends with Echo devices who are in your contacts book. The difference between a call and drop-in is how the person at the other end responds.

A call has to be answered, making it useful for talking to a friend over the internet; all of their Echo devices will ring (bar those set to Do Not Disturb).

Drop-ins are automatically connected, making the Echo a useful intercom system for the home, or just to see what's going on at home when you're out. Drop-in settings are managed by device. By default, drop-in is only enabled for members of your household and contacts with permission, but you can change that to only household members, or disable the feature entirely.

Amazon also has Announcements, where you can transmit a voice message to all Echo devices in your home ("Alexa, announce dinner is ready"). If you want to get the kids' attention, then it's a handy tool and matches Google Home's Broadcast feature.

Call quality, both audio and video, is excellent. I find it particularly useful in-house as a way to talk to other people when I'm too lazy to stand up and move. A recent update lets you make calls or drop in from the Alexa app on your phone or tablet, too.

With the Skype integration, you can hook your Alexa speakers up to your VoIP account and make calls. These can either be over the internet (Skype-to-Skype) or telephone calls using your Skype credit. That's not quite as powerful as the free landline and mobile calls that Google gives you with the Google Home.

You also can't set the outbound caller ID to match that of your mobile phone, as you can with Google. The nearest option is to buy a number from Skype and make out-bound calls from this. Alexa can call anyone in your Skype address book, although you can manually say a number to call, too. It's a shame that you can't just say the name of local business.

Common Amazon Echo problems – and how to fix them quickly

The Amazon Echo speaker range is hugely popular, with many houses having multiple speakers now. Although our experiences with the Alexa-enabled devices have been pain-free thus far, here are some of the Amazon Echo problems you may experience, complete with suggestions for how to resolve them.

The Wi-Fi connection is inconsistent or non-existent

Echo's connectivity status is indicated by the power LED on the bottom rear of the device, with white meaning good and orange denoting no Wi-Fi connectivity.

If you're experiencing intermittent connectivity or non-existent Wi-Fi connectivity with your Amazon Echo, here's what to try.

First, follow the usual drill: reboot your router and turn your Echo off and on again.

If that doesn't help and everything else on the network is working well, you might want to think about repositioning your Echo away from devices that may be interfering with the signal.

You can also reduce the congestion on your Wi-Fi network by removing unused devices from the network.

If you have a dual-band modem, you may effectively have two networks set up. Try switching the device from the 2.4GHz frequency to the 5GHz frequency or vice-versa. 5GHz promises less interference, better speeds and a more stable connection and it is often less congested.

Alternatively, 2.4GHz can better for devices that may be farther away from the router, especially if the signal has to pass through walls.

Move your Echo to higher ground, like a bookshelf, to avoid signal interference.

Alexa won't connect to other devices

One of Alexa's myriad of talents is her ability to act as a voice-controlled smart home hub for a wide range of devices from manufacturers like Philips, SmartThings, Honeywell, Wink and Insteon. However, discovery and connection isn't always smooth sailing.

Firstly, make sure your device is actually compatible with the Echo. It may need a bridge like the SmartThings or Wink hub. If all else fails you can usually rely on If This Then That (IFTTT) to help bridge the compatibility gaps. There's even an official Alexa IFTTT channel.

The next step, of course, is to follow the set-up instructions for the smart home device before asking Alexa to discover it. You may need to download a companion app and go through the motions.

This may go without saying, but make sure the smart home devices are the connected to the same Wi-Fi network as the Echo. If devices in your house have a habit of defaulting to the BT Openzone hotspot within your router, this will cause problems.

Also, ensure you've downloaded the most recent firmware and software updates for your devices, and remember that many smart home devices require you to enable it as a 'skill' in the Alexa app.

Open the app, hit the menu and select 'Skills' then search or search for the relevant manufacturer. Other devices, like Philips Hue, don't require a 'Skill' and can be linked just by asking Alexa to "Discover devices" while pressing the button on the Philips Hue bridge.

The Alexa app enables you to link smart home devices in a Group. This way you can use voice controls to control multiple devices with a single command, such as "turn off bedroom lights."

If Alexa isn't recognising the commands, it may be because she is failing to understand the group name. Change it to something easily discernible and speak it clearly.

Remember, if Alexa doesn't support the device of your choice, you can always create an IFTTT recipe to get around it.

Alexa doesn't understand me

"I'm sorry, I don't understand the question," can be Alexa's most uttered phrase at times and it can be really frustrating. Alexa's voice recognition naturally improves as it gets to know you, but there are ways to avoid repeating yourself.

Start by using the voice training tool. Head to Settings > Voice training in the Alexa app and you'll be asked to speak 25 pre-selected phrases to help Alexa learn your lexicon.

Next, check what Alexa actually heard. The Alexa app keeps a note of all of your requests, so you can see exactly what she heard. Go to the app's Settings and hit History. Here you can identify common misheard words and perhaps express them more clearly.

Finally, note your position. Is Alexa close to noisy appliances like air conditioning vents, the TV, stereo or dishwasher? Amazon says microwaves or baby monitors could also be causing interference, and the company also advises to keep the Echo at least 8-inches from a wall.

Alexa won't connect to my Bluetooth devices

The Echo supports the Advanced Audio Distribution Profile (A2DP SNK) and Audio / Video Remote Control Profile (AVRCP) so ensure the device you're attempting to connect matches up. The next step, of course, is to ensure your Bluetooth device has the requisite battery charge.

If you're still experiencing problems, you can un-pair and re-pair your Bluetooth devices. Open the Alexa app and hit Settings. Tap on your Echo device, select Bluetooth and Clear all paired devices.

To re-pair the devices, say "Pair" around Alexa to place the Echo in discovery mode. Next, head to the Bluetooth settings on your device or app in order to pair, as normal. Alexa will confirm the connection.

Streaming services aren't ... streaming

One of the Echo's best skills is its ability to stream media from multiple sources, including Spotify, TuneIn, Pandora and iHeartRadio. However, if you're experiencing intermittent performance, it's likely down to Wi-Fi interference. If that's the problem, follow the steps outlined above.

Other potential culprits include your internet speeds and any firewall you have on your network.

If your connection is less than 0.5Mbps, you're probably out of luck when it comes to effective streaming, while Amazon advises you to ensure the following ports are open if you're running additional security measures:

123, 443, 4070, 5353, 40317, 49317, 33434.

Reducing unwanted activations

On WWE Smackdown, there's a new-ish character called Alexa Bliss, who keeps waking our Echo. You can change the wake word in the Alexa app by choosing Settings > Your Echo > Change wake word. Unfortunately, the only other choices are the rather un-fun "Amazon" and "Echo".

Of course, you can always hit the microphone button on the top of the Echo in order to temporarily prevent her from eavesdropping on your conversations and TV shows.

Alexa Skills are playing up

Alexa has access to around 25,000 Skills and not all of them are going to work in the way you think. If a particular Skill isn't doing what it's told, it may just be a bad Apple. However, some might need a little finagling into proper performance. Namely by disabling and re-abling.

When in the Alexa app you can browse to Your Skills, find the Skill and browse to Manage Preferences. You can toggle these on and off. This may resolve the issue.

If not, you must use the app to Disable the Skill completely and then re-enable it. Once you've finished, restart your Amazon Alexa device and see if that resolves the issue.

All my Sonos speakers duck when I speak to Alexa

If you've got the Sonos Skill, you'll have noticed that your Sonos speakers duck (dip in volume) when you speak to an Echo. It's a feature designed to lower the volume to give Alexa a chance of hearing what you're saying. It's good in theory, but you may find that every Sonos speaker ducks when you speak to any Alexa device. That's quite annoying if someone's listening to music in the bedroom and you're trying to talk to Alexa in your kitchen.

The solution is to create Amazon Alexa groups. Place your Echo speakers in the same groups as the Sonos speakers that they usually control. For example, you group the kitchen Sonos and Echo together. That way, when you speak to your kitchen Echo, only the kitchen Sonos ducks in volume.

There are some minor issues with this. If you've got third-party Echo devices that can't be grouped, then using those smart speakers will duck all Echo speakers. Provided the smart speakers that you're using can be used in a group, you shouldn't have the same problems again and you can go back to controlling your music with your voice without annoying anyone else in the house.

If all else fails...

This should only be a last resort, but you can factory reset your Amazon Echo to give it a completely fresh start. There's a reset button next to the power adapter. You'll need to use a pin (or something equally small and pointy). Hold the button in until the light ring turns orange and you're good to go. The only problem is you'll have to set up the Echo all over again

Thank you for purchasing this book, I believe you have learned some tips and tricks that will help you to master your echo devices like a pro.